STRANGE UNSOLVED MYSTERIES
MYSTERIES OF SHIPS and PLANES

PHYLLIS RAYBIN EMERT

Strange Unsolved Mysteries from Tor Books

Mysteries of Ships and Planes
Monsters, Strange Dreams, and UFOs

STRANGE UNSOLVED MYSTERIES
MYSTERIES OF SHIPS and PLANES

PHYLLIS RAYBIN EMERT

TOR

A TOM DOHERTY ASSOCIATES BOOK
NEW YORK

MYSTERIES OF SHIPS AND PLANES

Copyright © 1990 by RGA Publishing Group, Inc.

A Tor Book
Published by Tom Doherty Associates, Inc.
49 West 24th Street
New York, N.Y. 10010

Cover art and interior illustrations by Paul Jennis

ISBN: 0-812-59427-4

First edition: October 1990

Printed in the United States of America

0 9 8 7 6 5 4 3 2 1

The author would like to thank
LARRY EMERT
for his continuous help and support

Contents

Andy Letchemy

❧ 1864 ❦

"Will you look at that, Captain," said the first mate who pointed to the northeast.

"It's a waterspout and a queer-looking thing," declared the captain. "She's a huge one. I'd say about ten miles away. Nothing to worry about, mate. We're going west and she's to the east."

The captain went below deck to eat his breakfast and attend to some paperwork.

Waterspouts are tornadoes at sea. Sometimes they happen in inland bodies of water like lakes or rivers. The funnel-shaped cloud extends down to the surface where heavy winds pick up the water and whirl it around at high speeds.

The skipper of the *Andy Letchemy*, a 150-ton vessel, was transporting laborers from one city to another off the coast of British-occupied India. It was the morning of March 15, 1864, when the waterspout was first sighted.

Sometime later when the captain came back on

deck he was startled to see that the giant column of water was much closer.

"Put her about!" he shouted to the crew. "I want some distance between that thing and us!"

The *Andy Letchemy* changed directions and so did the waterspout.

"It's no use, Captain! It's following us!" shouted the mate.

"It's not possible," answered the skipper, who frantically began turning the ship away from its watery pursuer.

But his efforts were in vain. Wherever the captain turned the *Andy Letchemy*, the waterspout seemed to follow.

"It's like the thing is alive, Captain," screamed the panicked mate, "and hunting us down!"

In the end, the ship was sucked into the whirling column. It was lifted right out of the sea and then thrown into the shrieking foamy water of the spout.

The *Andy Letchemy* disappeared from sight instantly, gobbled up by the waterspout. All but 7 of the 134 people who were on board went to their deaths.

The seven who escaped being sucked into the funnel were able to keep afloat by hanging on to pieces of the wreckage. Eventually, a passing ship rescued them from the sea.

Some of the survivors claim the waterspout was an evil force which set out to destroy the *Andy Letchemy*. Others feel its strange movements were just a coincidence mixed with bad luck. Bad luck or evil force? It will always be a mystery.

CF-100

✺ 1960 ✺

The air base traffic controller watched his radar screen carefully. Two Canadian jets were on a routine mission over Lake Ontario. They showed up as two blips on the lower portion of the screen.

Reaching for some report forms on the next desk, the controller turned his head for an instant. A moment later, he stared back at the screen. One of the blips was gone.

"Did you see that? It vanished off the screen," he said out loud. The other controllers had seen it too.

"This is CX-622 calling base control. I have a problem here," said the pilot. "This may be hard to believe but my lead plane has just disappeared. Please confirm. Over."

"Base to CX-622. He's disappeared from our radar also. Try to give us a position where he may have gone down. Over."

At first, it was thought the plane had suddenly

crashed. Perhaps, it had unexpected mechanical problems. But why didn't the pilot signal he was having difficulty?

It was September 1960. The two planes were CF-100 jets of the Canadian Armed Forces. As they flew across the sky through the clouds, the lead jet vanished into thin air.

After the pilot confirmed that the plane had also disappeared on the radar screens, he circled back to search for it. Perhaps he could find a parachute where the airman ejected from the plane.

But nothing was found. There was no smoke, wreckage, or parachute. The only trace of the CF-100 was the streaks of condensed vapor left by all aircraft at high altitudes. And those streaks stopped suddenly where the plane had disappeared.

The pilot returned to base and rescue teams began to search the countryside for wreckage and witnesses. No one saw a plane go down and nothing unusual was discovered on the ground.

Next, they searched Lake Ontario which is no deeper than two hundred feet. Within several miles of the shore, the depth is less than a hundred feet. If the CF-100 went down in the lake, it could easily be spotted.

But nothing was found in the lake. The currents are mild, so wreckage and other remains of the plane wouldn't be carried away.

The Canadian Defense Department closed the file on the missing airplane and its pilot—whereabouts unknown.

How did the airplane vanish in full view without a trace? Did a mysterious force snatch it out of the sky? Did it fly through an opening into another dimension? Did it go forward or backward into time? Until any evidence is found, the file will remain closed.

Octavius

❧ 1775 ❧

All through the night, gale force winds tore at the whaling ship, *Herald*. Sailing from Greenland in 1775, the ship was in polar arctic waters, traveling among the icebergs and ice floes.

When the storm began, the crew was afraid they'd be trapped in the ice. But it passed and finally the sun rose over the blinding white landscape.

"Ship off to starboard," shouted the lookout excitedly as a vessel glided into view from behind an iceberg.

"She's covered with ice," remarked the captain as it came closer to the *Herald*. "No signs of life aboard," he said.

He was able to read the name printed on the stern (rear) of the ship. "Ahoy, *Octavius*." There was no answer. The ice made the ship sparkle in the bright sunlight.

"Looks like a derelict. Let's board her," declared the captain.

On the deck of the deserted ship, there was drifting snow everywhere, but no one in sight.

The men went below deck after forcing open ice-sealed doors. In the crew's quarters, they discovered about twenty-eight men, bundled up in clothing and blankets—frozen to death!

The extreme cold had preserved the bodies so well that they looked very much like they did when they were alive.

The crewmen of the *Herald* were uneasy. "Let's check the captain's quarters," said their own skipper.

They found the body of the captain of the *Octavius* still sitting at a table in his cabin. The ship's log lay before him with a pen near one hand.

In a connecting cabin, the captain's wife lay dead in bed. Nearby, a man had frozen to death while trying to light a fire. The body of a young boy was found in a fur coat.

The figures all seemed alive and the crewmen were filled with fear. Captain Warren wanted to inspect the ship's cargo but his crew was anxious to leave the eerie death ship as soon as possible.

The captain took the ship's log as they hurriedly left and returned to the *Herald*. The crew watched in silence as the strange vessel drifted into the distance until they could no longer see it.

From the log, Captain Warren found out that the *Octavius* left England for the Orient in 1761. The captain brought his wife and ten-year-old son along. There were twenty-nine crewmen aboard.

Apparently they reached their destination and were returning to England in 1762. Most ships traveled around Cape Horn, at the lower tip of South America, to get from the Pacific to the Atlantic Ocean. It was a long and often dangerous journey.

The captain of the *Octavius* decided to look for a passageway home to England in the north though others had tried but failed before him. If successful, it would save hundreds of miles and many weeks at sea. But it was a great risk.

According to the log, dated November 1762, the *Octavius* became locked in ice in the Arctic Ocean, north of what is now Alaska. At the time of the log entry, they had been trapped for seventeen days and had no fire or warmth. The captain's son had died and the crewmen were in poor condition and near death.

The *Herald* came upon the *Octavius* in 1775 in the North Atlantic off Greenland, thirteen years *after* the crew and passengers had frozen to death. The ship had broken free of the ice and drifted through the passageway its captain had hoped to find in 1762.

Why did the captain take the risk of finding a northwest passage when others had failed? No one will ever know. The *Octavius* and its lifeless crew was never seen again.

Boelcke's Derelict

✿ 1916 ✿

World War I was in full swing in September 1916. Dogfights between two or more fighter planes flying close to each other was a common sight.

One dawn morning, two airmen from the Australian Flying Corps took off on a mission over no-man's-land (the battleground between the German armies and the British and French forces). Lieutenant Sandy, the pilot, and Sergeant Hughes, the wireless operator, were supposed to direct ground artillery to German positions.

Suddenly, a squadron of German fighters came out of the clouds and attacked the Australians. Two other planes came to their rescue and there was a dogfight.

One of the German planes was shot down. The others flew off. The two rescue planes waved good-bye to Sandy and Hughes and then went on their way.

A short time later, Captain Oswald Boelcke, a

top German pilot, was flying home to Germany after a dawn raid over France. Five other German planes were with him including Baron von Richthofen, who later was known as the Red Baron.

Suddenly a British plane flew out of the clouds directly at the Germans. The squadron scattered. One by one, the German pilots attacked the plane. They poured round after round of machine gun fire into the body of the aircraft and the cockpit where the crew sat.

"Why are they holding their fire?" thought Boelcke to himself. "They just keep flying on." He waved his men off. "I'll finish the job myself."

Boelcke swept down on the British plane, aimed his machine guns into the cockpit, and let loose with a burst of bullets. But still the plane flew on, apparently unaffected. Boelcke clearly saw his bullets go into the aircraft. "It's impossible," he thought.

Slowly, the German ace flew closer to the mysterious airplane. Only a few yards separated them now. Boelcke stared into the cockpit.

What he saw made him shiver with fear. There strapped and sitting upright in their seats were the dead bodies of Sandy and Hughes, smeared with blood. They stared straight ahead as if they were still at the controls of the death plane.

Boelcke flew along with them for a while. Then he dipped his wings, saluted, and left to join the others. When they returned home, Boelcke wrote about the incident in his flight report. He believed the men were already dead when they flew out of the clouds. A month later, Boelcke died in combat.

What happened to the death plane? It flew on

for almost an hour until it ran out of fuel. It silently glided forward and, by some mysterious force of its own, made a smooth landing in a field in France.

French soldiers carried the dead bodies to a nearby hospital. Doctors found that both men had been killed by a bullet which first went through Hughes's chest and then came to a stop in Sandy's brain. They had died in an instant and were dead for more than an hour when the plane landed.

The aircraft itself was full of bullet holes. Yet, not one shot had hit the propeller, engine, or gas tank.

How did the plane, with two dead men at the controls, make it home from enemy territory? How was it able to land safely? No one knows.

Mary Celeste

❧ 1872 ❧

Some sailors believe that certain ships are just "born unlucky." The *Mary Celeste* was one of these. Many called her a jinx ship.

Built in 1861, the 103-foot, two-masted British sailing ship was originally named the *Amazon*. Her captain died shortly after taking command.

On her first voyage, she damaged her hull. While being repaired, a fire broke out. During an Atlantic crossing, she collided with another ship. By this time, the unlucky *Amazon* had had four captains.

In 1867 she ran aground off Nova Scotia. Her ownership changed hands several times. After being repaired and sold to an American, her name was changed to *Mary Celeste*.

Many sailors refused to serve on the *Mary Celeste*. They felt it was unlucky to change a ship's name. The 282-ton vessel switched owners several more times. Finally, Benjamin Briggs became her captain and part-owner.

The *Mary Celeste* was due to sail from New York Harbor on November 5, 1872. She carried a cargo of seventeen hundred barrels of alcohol and was bound for Genoa, Italy.

Briggs's friend, Captain David Morehouse, of the *Dei Gratia*, was headed for Gibraltar. The two had dinner together and wished each other well.

Two days later Briggs set sail followed by Morehouse in the *Dei Gratia* the next week. Captain Briggs brought along his wife, Sarah, and his baby daughter. He was an experienced skipper looking forward to an uneventful journey.

On December 5, the two ships met six hundred miles from Portugal in the mid-Atlantic.

"Ship off the port bow!" shouted the lookout on the *Dei Gratia*.

Captain Morehouse took a look with his eyeglasses. "Why, it's the *Mary Celeste*," he declared, "and there's no one at the wheel or on deck."

Some of her sails appeared torn and the ship looked out of control.

Morehouse sent over a boarding party who searched the vessel thoroughly. They had disturbing news. Not a soul was on board. The *Mary Celeste* was deserted.

The cargo was in place but one of the containers had been opened. The lifeboat was missing. The crew must have left in a hurry in the boat since they hadn't taken their personal belongings with them.

In the captain's cabin, the strongbox was still locked. The last entry in the log was dated November 24, and recorded the ship's position as 110 miles west of the Azores.

The captain's bed was unmade. Some toys and sewing articles were found. A bottle of medicine was open with the spoon nearby. There was plenty of food and drinking water in the galley (a six-month supply).

There was nothing wrong with the ship itself. She was completely seaworthy and in good condition.

There were no signs of violence or robbery anywhere. The only thing missing from the *Mary Celeste* was the ship's papers and some navigation books and equipment.

Captain Morehouse decided to claim the *Mary Celeste* as salvage and towed her in to the port at Gibraltar.

During the Admiralty Court investigation which followed, some suspected Captain Morehouse of foul play. They felt murder had been committed so he could collect the salvage money. But the naval court cleared Morehouse and his men from any wrongdoing.

The court never did reach a conclusion as to what happened to the crew of the *Mary Celeste*. In the years that passed, the mystery grew and facts were changed to add a touch of drama to the story.

Actually, there were no tables set with uneaten food on board. Coffee and tea were not discovered steaming in their cups. There was no blood-stained sword and no page of the logbook was missing.

Some believed that the *Mary Celeste* was attacked by a giant squid or octopus which plucked each person off the ship one by one.

Others felt that all were drowned while watching a swimming race around the ship between the captain and the mate. They had been sitting on a platform under the bow and it collapsed into the water.

Still others insisted that the crew had drunk the alcohol, gone crazy, and killed everyone on board.

The *Mary Celeste* was in good condition apart from some torn sails, so a terrible storm or the fear of sinking wasn't the reason for abandoning the ship.

Three facts stand out: (1) the ship was abandoned quickly, (2) they left in the lifeboat, (3) they took navigation equipment and the ship's papers with them.

The most likely answer to the mystery of the *Mary Celeste* concerns her cargo of alcohol. Perhaps, the barrels gave off fumes and Captain Briggs feared the ship would explode since alcohol burns so easily.

He might have ordered all hands, including his family, into the lifeboat to see what would happen. When Briggs decided to return to the ship, a wind came up blowing the *Mary Celeste* far away from the boat. The crew rowed and rowed but they couldn't catch up with the ship. All ten aboard were stranded far from land and were eventually swamped by rough waves. It may have happened this way but can never be proven.

The story doesn't end in 1873. The *Mary Celeste* was sold again and again and continued to sail under other captains. Finally in 1884, Captain Gilman Parker wrecked the ship on a coral reef near Haiti for the insurance money. When it didn't break up, he burned it to the ground. But Parker was never allowed to collect the money. He died eight months later in poverty.

Flight 19

❧ 1945 ❧

The mysterious disappearance of Flight 19 has been called the *"Mary Celeste* of the sky." At 2:10 P.M. on December 5, 1945, five single-engine Avenger torpedo bombers took off from the Naval Air Station at Fort Lauderdale, Florida. It was a routine training patrol scheduled to last about two hours.

The planes were supposed to fly 56 miles east to practice low-level bombing runs. Then they would fly north 73 miles over Grand Bahama Island, and finally 120 miles west back to Fort Lauderdale.

The five planes carried fourteen men. Lieutenant Charles Taylor was the instructor on the flight. All but two of the crew were students in training. The Avengers had self-inflating life rafts and each man wore a life jacket.

Five hours after they took off, the pilots and their planes vanished without a trace! Years later, it was reported that the flight leader said, "Everything is wrong ... strange ... we can't be sure of

any direction. Even the ocean doesn't look as it should!"

A rescue plane, a Martin Mariner flying boat with a crew of thirteen, was part of the search team. It, too, disappeared without a trace.

One naval officer was reported to have said, "They vanished as completely as if they'd flown to Mars. We don't know what's . . . going on out there."

Some said that all six planes were victims of the mysterious area of water known as the Bermuda Triangle. Perhaps UFOs or strange unearthly forces were responsible for their disappearance?

But many of these quotes were false. Taylor never said, ". . . the ocean doesn't look as it should!" A navy officer didn't say anything about Mars. What really was said is noted in the Navy investigation report on the incident.

About 1½ hours into the flight, one of the training pilots said, "I don't know where we are. We must have got lost after that last turn."

Later Taylor said, "Both my compasses are out . . . I'm sure I'm in the Keys . . . I don't know how to get to Fort Lauderdale." Taylor was advised to try to fly north. Then he replied, "I know where I am now . . . Don't come after me."

At about 5:15 P.M. radio contact began to fade and Taylor was asked to switch to the emergency frequency channel. He refused, saying, "I can't change frequency. I must keep my planes intact."

Then Taylor told the pilots to keep flying in formation. If any one plane had to ditch, they would ditch together. The five planes only had enough fuel to last until 8:00 P.M. After dark, the weather turned very rough.

Meanwhile the Miami Coast Guard and other communications centers were trying to pinpoint their position. Until they had a position fix on the missing aircraft, the Navy didn't want to send a rescue plane out in the dark in bad weather.

At 6 P.M. the ComGulf Sea Frontier Evaluation Center in Miami computed a general position for Flight 19 from radio messages overheard. They were actually east of Florida and hundreds of miles north of the Bahamas. Taylor had mistakenly thought he was over the Florida Keys. By flying north, he was over the Atlantic when he thought he was over the Gulf of Mexico.

At around 6:15 Taylor was heard to say to the other pilots, "I suggest we fly due east until we run out of gas. We have a better chance of being picked up close to shore."

Actually, Taylor was flying deeper into the Atlantic and away from shore! But no one tried to tell him of his actual position once it was known. Two-way communication was very bad and the signal was fading in and out.

The last message from any of the pilots on Flight 19 was at 7:04 P.M. Rescue planes took to the air around that time. One of them, a Martin Mariner, disappeared suddenly and could not be contacted. A ship, the SS *Gaines Mill*, reported seeing a plane catch fire and then a flaming explosion at sea in the area where the Martin Mariner was supposed to be. They spotted a large oil slick and debris but couldn't retrieve the wreckage because of the rough sea.

The next day, a full-scale search began involving hundreds of ships and planes. After five days, no wreckage, debris, or bodies from Flight 19 could be found.

If Taylor's compasses were out, he wouldn't have known what direction he had been flying or which way to go. (Whether the student pilot's compasses were working is not known.) But Taylor thought he was over the Florida Keys when he was really far off course.

The actions he took only seemed to add to his confusion. He and the rest of the men were totally lost. They couldn't seem to find a way out of the situation.

If Taylor had switched to the emergency frequency channel, two-way communication would have been clear. But he was afraid that one or more of the other planes wouldn't be able to pick up the new frequency, and he would lose contact with them.

Flight 19 kept trying to find their way home, but they eventually ran out of fuel. Together they ditched into a very rough and stormy sea.

The Avenger could stay afloat for only fifteen to twenty seconds. In total darkness, with icy seawater pouring in, the men would have had to escape from the plane, pull the raft from its compartment, jump away from the sinking plane, and inflate the raft.

It's possible that the planes quickly sank, along with the bodies and any debris from the craft, especially in such stormy weather. By the next morning, when the full-scale search began, not a trace of Flight 19 was left.

The Martin Mariner rescue plane carried almost two thousand gallons of fuel. It apparently exploded in the air, as witnessed by those aboard the *Gaines Mill*.

There are still unanswered questions about Flight 19. Why didn't the Navy send several rescue planes out sooner to cover a number of possible search areas? Perhaps, they could have established clearer radio contact with the lost flight and been able to pinpoint their position sooner?

Why didn't anyone contact Taylor and attempt to give him their actual position once it was known? If Taylor had known at 6:00 P.M. that they were east of Florida and so far north, he might have turned toward shore with two hours of fuel still left.

One thing is known for sure. On December 5, 1945, the men of Flight 19 flew into aviation history forever.

Eleanor Hamilton

❧ 1854 ❧

"I've got a funny feeling about this trip, mate,"
said the sailor. "Like something's out there just
waiting for us."

"Nonsense," his friend replied. "You're being
ridiculous and getting the other men nervous."

"They feel the same as I do," he declared. "Mark
my words. We're heading for our doom if we sail
on schedule."

The year was 1854. The ship was the *Eleanor
Hamilton*. It was fall, and the crew was preparing
for a voyage down Lake Ontario through the
Marysburgh Vortex. The Vortex was an area of
water at the eastern end of the lake that had a
history of shipwrecks and strange happenings.

"The men are afraid to sail, Captain. They've
had bad dreams and strange feelings about the
voyage," said the first mate.

"Maybe it's something they ate," replied the
captain. "Some underdone meat? Or too much

plum pudding, perhaps? Don't be silly. The preparations for our voyage will continue."

"Sir, could we postpone the trip, just for a few days," the first mate pleaded.

"Absolutely not! Just tell them there's no power on the face of this earth that can hurt this ship!" declared the captain.

Finally the work was finished and the *Eleanor Hamilton* prepared to get underway.

"Cast off lines," shouted the first mate. The crew was strangely quiet as they glided slowly out of port. For once, even the captain was speechless.

The *Eleanor Hamilton* and her crew were never seen again.

Days later, wreckage from the ship began to wash ashore. There were bits and pieces of the hull, deck, and cabins. The masts appeared to be sliced off in pieces. Something terrible and violent had happened to the *Eleanor Hamilton*. One person said it was as if "a giant fist had slammed down on the vessel."

The ship was broken into pieces, but what happened to the crew? No bodies washed ashore nor were any ever found. The men had vanished.

How did the crew know in advance that something terrible would happen? Were they taken off the ship *before* it was crushed? If so, where did they go? What could have caused such wreckage? There were no reported storms in the area.

The captain bragged that nothing on earth could harm his ship. If it wasn't a power on earth, then what was it?

USS *Memphis*

❧ 1916 ❦

It was a beautiful summer day in Santo Domingo on the southern coast of the Dominican Republic. The sea was calm and there wasn't a cloud in the bright, blue sky. The air was still. Not even a slight breeze was blowing.

It was August 29, 1916. American Marines assigned to Santo Domingo were protecting United States interests in the small republic. They were there to keep the peace and make sure the government stayed honest.

Two U.S. Navy ships, the cruiser *Memphis* and the gunboat *Castine*, were anchored in the harbor. Both ships were powered by steam engines which were fueled by coal.

It was a relaxing day. Sailors from the *Memphis* went ashore to play baseball. Commander Bennett of the *Castine* was having lunch with Captain Beach on board the *Memphis*.

Around midday the waves began to swell slightly. As the hours went by, the height of the waves increased but this wasn't noticed in the harbor where the ships were anchored. The sea was smooth. The skies were cloudless and there was barely a breeze.

The *Memphis* started to roll more noticeably and Captain Bennett decided to return to the *Castine*. A boat was sent from the *Memphis* to pick up some of the sailors on shore.

The sea looked calm but the ships were rolling much more than usual. Both captains ordered their boilers to be fired up and soon, black smoke erupted from the stacks of the *Castine*.

In the *Memphis*, the men had problems lighting the boilers. The ship's rolling was now so great that they had trouble keeping the water level in the boilers and placing the hot coals in the fire boxes under them.

Up on the bridge of the *Memphis*, Captain Beach stood with his first officer, Lieutenant Commander Williams. The captain looked out to sea. The waters still seemed calm.

"My God, where's the horizon?" he whispered in horror.

Instead of the horizon, all Beach and Williams could see was a giant wall of water, almost one hundred feet high. A monster wave was bearing down on them.

"Man your stations!" shouted the captain. "Secure for heavy weather!"

On the *Castine*, waves started to break over the decks. The men tried to bring up the anchor but couldn't. The bow of the ship rose thirty feet out of the water and then dropped back down again.

"Up anchor, up anchor," Commander Bennett

yelled. Slowly and with much difficulty, the anchor was lifted.

By now waves were crashing down on the decks of the *Memphis*, forcing water into the fire and engine rooms below. The boilers were flooded and the men were thrown around by the rolling of the waves.

On the bridge, the captain saw the giant wave was a mile away and moving in fast. But still there was no wind and the sky remained cloudless.

The boat, sent from the *Memphis*, was now returning from shore loaded with thirty-one sailors. They got caught in the waves and couldn't get back.

The pounding water finally overwhelmed them and all on board were thrown into the churning sea. Afraid that the out-of-control ship would run over these sailors, the *Castine* headed out to sea and was able to climb over the giant wave with power from her engines.

On the *Memphis*, men and loose objects on deck were being washed overboard by the higher and higher waves. The boilers couldn't be lit. The engines couldn't get steam.

The increasing waves were forcing the bottom of the *Memphis* against the sea floor, damaging her hull plates. The ship which was normally thirty feet in the water was hitting the bottom in fifty-five feet of water.

Lifeboats were smashed. The anchor couldn't stop the *Memphis* from moving closer and closer to shore. The giant wave, higher than the smokestacks, poured over the ship. The men below were thrown against walls and scorched by steam lines.

The bottom of the eighteen-thousand-ton ship ground against the sea floor loudly. Then the bow came up high out of the water and crashed down again. Each new wave brought the *Memphis* closer to the rocks lining the harbor.

Marines still on shore watched in horror. The summer sun beat down out of the blue sky. There was only a slight breeze. But the water was churning. The ship seemed lost.

At 5:00 P.M. the *Memphis* smashed into the sea floor and stayed there. Her bottom was ripped away. She was one hundred feet from the rocks of the bluff. They would have broken her to pieces.

Miraculously, the ship stayed upright and the crewmen were removed by lifelines. Captain Beach was the last man to leave.

The *Castine* returned to the harbor the next day, heavily damaged. The *Memphis* was aground, a battered and dead ship. The giant wave had killed forty-six sailors and injured many more.

The mystery continued when several days later two men from a salvage crew had a strange experience. They were searching one of the lower decks when they heard a groaning sound all around them.

"It's just the movement of the ship in the water," said one.

They moved to the next compartment. Shining their lantern ahead, they saw what appeared to be a pale face of a seaman. Both men saw it and both men ran away quickly, very frightened.

Other members of the salvage crew later saw one or two of these "ghost" faces. Some swore it was two of the *Memphis*'s crew who had died.

Others said the men were really alive and had deserted. But no one knows for sure and probably never will.

Where did the death wave come from? Some said it was caused by an earthquake or undersea volcano.

It just came out of nowhere so suddenly on that beautiful summer day.

Star Tiger

❧ 1948 ❧

"We've got a few interesting passengers on this flight," declared Lynn Clayton. She and Sheila Nicholls were stewardesses in January 1948. (The British called them air hostesses.)

They were also known as "Star Girls" because the first three planes that flew the brand-new route from London, England to Havana, Cuba were named *Star Panther, Star Lion,* and *Star Tiger.*

"I know, Lynn. I've already met Air Marshal Coningham," replied Sheila. "And Mr. Brooks is the Assistant Secretary of the Treasury."

The Avro Tudor *Star* aircraft began service in 1947 with British South American Airways. First, they flew from London to Lisbon, Portugal. Then, they traveled from Lisbon to Santa Maria in the Azores (a group of Portuguese islands). Here the Tudor refueled and set off for Bermuda. And finally, they flew into Havana, their destination.

The flight from the Azores to Bermuda was the longest ocean crossing for any commercial airline. The route was nearly two thousand miles of ocean, passing over no land at all. There were no weather ships and few vessels of any kind in this area of the Atlantic. Weather information wasn't always accurate, especially about the strong head-winds on the route.

These heavy winds could blow a plane off course, slow it down, and eat up fuel. One Tudor aircraft landed in Bermuda with its fuel gauge actually on empty. The plane came very close to ditching in the sea.

The Star Girls, Lynn and Sheila, were working the flight of the *Star Tiger* when it left London Airport on January 27. Captain Brian McMillan was the pilot, assisted by copilot David Colby.

After arrival in Lisbon, the flight to the Azores was delayed for minor repairs until the next morning. When Captain McMillan finally arrived at Santa Maria there was a sixty-knot wind. (A knot is equal to one nautical mile, which is the unit of distance used for sea and air navigation.) He decided to postpone the trip to Bermuda for twenty-four hours, hoping the winds would decrease.

Early the next morning, the winds died down and McMillan prepared for an afternoon flight. These flights always took off in mid- or late afternoon. The plane would be flying in darkness much of the time. This was done so the navigator could use the stars to get a fix on their position and determine wind strength.

The *Star Tiger* carried twenty-five passengers plus a crew of six. It left Santa Maria at 3:34 P.M. The flight was expected to take 12½ hours. The plane had about 3½ extra hours of fuel for an emergency.

Two hundred miles ahead of the *Star Tiger* on the Azores-to-Bermuda route was Captain Frank Griffin flying a Lancastrian cargo plane. Griffin relayed messages back to McMillan that the wind was now up to fifty-five knots. The planes would be delayed one hour.

Navigators on both aircraft had few chances of getting a star position fix since the sky was overcast and cloudy. But around 1:00 A.M. the weather cleared and Griffin's navigator discovered that the plane had been blown off course and the wind had changed directions.

Like Griffin's plane, the *Star Tiger* had also been blown off course. That meant still another hour of delay until they reached their destination. They were running out of their extra fuel.

At 3:00 A.M. Griffin was only an hour out and had switched to voice contact with the Bermuda Approach Control. "See you at breakfast" was his last message to McMillan.

At 3:15 A.M. because it was so overcast, the *Star Tiger* requested and was able to get a bearing on her position from the ground operator at Bermuda. Arrival time was now changed to 5:00 A.M.

This was the last communication anyone had with the *Star Tiger*, which was four hundred miles away from Bermuda. After unsuccessful attempts to contact the plane, the operator declared an emergency, ninety-five minutes after the last contact. Within hours, a search plane was in the air.

During the day, twenty-five other aircraft took part in the search. The weather got bad quickly with poor visibility and choppy waves. Over the next five days, not a trace of wreckage, oil slicks, debris, or bodies was found from the *Star Tiger*.

The plane was equipped with survival kits, rubber life rafts, and a small radio. If it went down and the passengers were able to get into the life rafts, it's unlikely they could have survived in such a rough sea or that wreckage would be found.

What really happened to the *Star Tiger*? Why wasn't a distress signal sent? Was there radio failure? Was there a mechanical or electrical breakdown on board?

The British Minister of Civil Aviation's report on the disappearance of the *Star Tiger* stated that radio failure was very unlikely. Even without a radio, a course set using the 3:15 A.M. bearing given by the ground operator would have brought the plane to within miles of Bermuda before running out of fuel.

The report also ruled out mechanical failure of the engines and constructional defects as the cause of the disappearance.

Was there a loss of control in the aircraft or a fire on board or perhaps both? These things weren't very likely. But they are all possibilities no matter how unlikely they seem.

The report ended by stating "What happened in this case will never be known and the fate of *Star Tiger* must forever remain a mystery."

Star Ariel

❧ 1949 ❧

Almost a year after the disappearance of the *Star Tiger*, another Tudor *Star* aircraft was making its regular run from London, England, to Santiago, Chile.

The *Star Ariel*, a British South American Airways plane, had flown without problems from London to Bermuda. The next part of the trip was from Bermuda to Kingston, Jamaica, and, after refueling, on to Santiago.

The four-engine Tudor took off from Kindley Field in Bermuda at 8:41 in the morning on January 17, 1949. The flight was expected to take 5½ hours and arrive in Kingston at about 2:10 in the afternoon. Captain J.C. McPhee, an experienced pilot, had enough fuel for ten hours of flying.

Thirteen passengers were on board the *Star Ariel*, including a two-year-old boy. There were six crew members. It was clear and sunny when the plane took off. The passengers could see for miles in all directions. The dark blue of the Atlantic

Ocean contrasted with the bright blue of the sky. It was perfect flying weather!

Fifty-one minutes after leaving Bermuda, Captain McPhee radioed a flight report to Kindley Field.

"I am flying in good visibility at eighteen thousand feet . . ."

Ten minutes later he stated, "I am changing frequency to Kingston." Then Bermuda signed off, assuming that all future radio messages would be with the airport in Jamaica.

Captain McPhee was only 150 miles out of Bermuda when he decided to communicate with Kingston, which was still 950 miles away. He had no radio contact with them yet since he wasn't close enough. Why did McPhee change his frequency to Kingston so early in the flight? Most pilots wait until the halfway point in the trip to switch frequencies.

Also, why didn't Bermuda question the change? Bermuda was responsible for keeping watch over the *Star Ariel* until the halfway point and until the aircraft had radio contact with Kingston.

As a result, Kingston didn't know that the *Star Ariel* had ended communications with Bermuda. And Bermuda didn't know that the plane hadn't contacted Kingston.

Four hours and ten minutes passed. Finally at 1:52 P.M., eighteen minutes before *Star Ariel* was due to arrive, Kingston radioed Bermuda, "Where is the *Star Ariel*? We've had no word since takeoff at 8:41 this morning."

Bermuda also had no contact with the *Star Ariel* since that last message at 9:42 A.M. An alert was sounded. At 2:45 P.M., the plane was listed as over-due. By the time a full search was ordered and underway, it was after dark.

The search lasted for five days. Planes and ships combed the sea between Bermuda, Kingston, and the eastern seaboard of the United States.

Like her sister ship, the *Star Tiger*, not a single trace of wreckage, bodies, or debris from the aircraft was ever found.

What happened to the *Star Ariel*? Why wasn't a distress signal sent, if the plane was in trouble? Did the *Star Ariel* crash in the sea and plunge directly to the bottom, taking everything and everyone with her? An investigation committee found that it would be almost impossible for such a large plane to have crashed without leaving debris on the surface.

Some people say it was sabotage (to destroy the aircraft on purpose). Did a bomb explode suddenly during the flight? If so, where were the pieces of the plane which would have scattered over a large area?

No one knows why Captain McPhee switched frequencies so early in the flight. But the delay in sounding an alert, after no contact with the plane for several hours, was an unexplained oversight by officials at the Bermuda and Kingston airports.

If the *Star Ariel* had gone down, it's possible that there may have been survivors. The aircraft had five emergency exits, carried three life rafts, a radio transmitter, and life belts. The late start in beginning the search may have been a factor in not finding survivors. But the weather was good and the sea calm. Surely, some trace of the aircraft or passengers should have been discovered even with the delay.

The investigator's report stated that the Tudor aircraft was not defective in any way. However, they were never used again to carry passengers after the disappearance of the *Star Tiger* and *Star Ariel*. This incident helped to bankrupt the airline which was taken over by another British air service in 1950.

If the airplane was in good running order, the weather perfect, and the pilot experienced, what happened to the *Star Ariel*? Some believe that other mysterious and unexplained forces were at work in the area around Bermuda!

The Chief Inspector of Accidents concluded: "Through lack of evidence due to no wreckage having been found, the cause of the accident is unknown."

James B. Chester

❧ 1855 ☙

The sea was rough on the morning of February 28, 1855. The small British trading ship, *Marathon*, was making its way through the waters of the middle-Atlantic. It was about six hundred miles southwest of the Azores.

Ocean crossings took many days. Meeting another ship in the huge Atlantic Ocean didn't happen very often. So when the lookout shouted, "Ship off the front bow," all hands took a look.

The captain on deck grabbed his glasses and saw a three-masted sailing vessel of about a thousand tons. (Masts are the poles rising up from the deck which help support the sails and lines.)

"She's been in bad weather," the captain remarked to his first mate, John Thomas. "Her riggings (lines) are tangled. And look at the way she's acting."

"Aye, Captain, she's swerving in one direction and then another," answered Thomas.

The crew of the *Marathon* had all gathered on

deck and were watching the strange ship. As it came closer, the captain used a megaphone to shout, "Ship ahoy. Identify yourself."

There was no answer. No one was on deck. "Something's wrong, sir," said Thomas.

If the ship was a derelict (abandoned by the crew) the captain had salvage rights to it. He would be paid for towing the vessel and its cargo to port.

"Take a boat and see what's going on," ordered the captain.

"Aye, aye, sir," replied the mate.

Soon, a boarding party was in the water. When they got closer to the ship, they could read its name clearly—the *James B. Chester*.

Everything was strangely quiet on deck as they looked around slowly. "There's nobody here," said Thomas.

"It's devil's work," one of the crew whispered.

Coils of rope were thrown around the deck and the sails were loose. Otherwise, everything seemed to be in good condition.

The men went below decks, one by one. The creaking of the ship and the water lapping against its side were the only sounds they heard.

The cabins were turned upside down. Tables and chairs were overturned. Drawers and clothes were thrown everywhere. But the cargo of wool and other supplies wasn't disturbed.

The ship's papers and compass were gone, but there were no bodies, blood, or weapons found. Food and water was plentiful and untouched. The ship's lifeboats were still in their proper places.

Thomas rowed back to the *Marathon* and reported to the captain. Then the deserted *James B. Chester* was towed into Liverpool as salvage.

No trace of the crew was ever found. If they had taken part in a mutiny against the captain and officers, there would have been signs of bloodshed.

If pirates had boarded the *James B. Chester*, there surely would have been a fight. Also, the pirates wouldn't have left the cargo untouched and then abandoned the ship.

All lifeboats were accounted for, so how did the crew leave the ship? Even if there had been an additional boat on board, experienced crewmen knew a small boat in the Atlantic couldn't last long in the stormy winter months.

Some superstitious seamen blame a sea serpent or sea monster for the crew's disappearance. But how could such a monster take the crew and leave the ship undamaged?

What caused the crew to leave the *James B. Chester* so quickly, making a mess of the cabins? There was plenty of food and water and the ship didn't appear to be in danger of sinking.

"Panic ... can account for it," said Elliot O'Donnell, in his book, *Strange Sea Mysteries*. "... Something occurred on board the *James B. Chester* that threw the crew ... into such a rare state of terror that they collected together a few valuables in the greatest haste ... and quitted the vessel in a body, preferring to run the risk of a watery grave, than to face ... they knew not what."

USS *Cyclops*

❧ 1918 ❧

The newspaper headline read "Big War Supply Ship Vanishes Without Trace."

Months later, the U.S. Navy declared, "The disappearance of this ship has been one of the most baffling mysteries in . . . the Navy."

President Woodrow Wilson stated, "Only God and the sea know what happened to the great ship."

The USS *Cyclops* was a 19,600-ton Navy collier, a ship used in transporting coal and ore.

Three hundred and nine people were aboard the *Cyclops* when it left Barbados in the West Indies on March 4, 1918. It was bound for Norfolk, Virginia with a cargo of ten thousand tons of manganese ore. This type of ore was used in the production of steel.

World War I was being fought in Europe. Some of the *Cyclops*'s cargo would be used to make weapons to fight against Germany in the war.

The 542-foot vessel, one of the largest at that

time, was only eight years old. It carried wireless radio equipment and lifeboats. One of her two engines was damaged so the *Cyclops* had to slow down her speed.

The last radio contact was on March 5, twenty-four hours after she left Barbados. The message reported fair weather and mentioned no problems.

Then the *Cyclops* vanished without a trace. It never arrived in Norfolk and no SOS or additional radio messages were ever sent.

The Navy searched the area but found nothing. On June 14, 1918, all Navy crew and passengers on the *Cyclops* were officially declared dead.

How could a ship of such size have disappeared so quickly, that an SOS couldn't have been sent? Why were there no bodies, or wreckage from the ship?

Many thought they had the answer to the mystery. The *Literary Digest* suggested that a giant squid had wrapped itself around the ship and pulled it to the bottom of the sea.

Some thought the Germans were responsible. They torpedoed the ship or took it over and sailed to Germany. But there was no wreckage found and the crew would not have given up without a fight or an SOS since America was at war with Germany.

The *Cyclops*'s captain, George W. Worley, had been born in Germany and changed his name from Wichman. But Captain Worley was a United States citizen and Navy veteran for twenty-eight years. He was a loyal American who, his wife said, "hated Germany."

Years later, after the war, the Germans declared they had nothing to do with the disappearance of the *Cyclops*.

Some believe the ship was top-heavy. The cargo shifted causing the *Cyclops* to overturn and sink immediately. But this could only happen in a bad storm. According to the Navy, the weather was reported to be good along the route.

More than half a century has passed and the mystery still remains. In 1968 a Navy diver discovered a wreck in 180 feet of water, only seventy miles from Norfolk. The diver was positive that it was the *Cyclops* but wasn't able to find it again.

One author and researcher, Larry Kusche, checked weather reports for the Norfolk area around March 10, 1918. Gale force winds were blowing from the north at sixty miles per hour. They could have been much worse at sea.

Perhaps the *Cyclops* was near the *end* of her voyage when disaster struck? Kusche believes the Navy thought the ship had been lost at the beginning of the trip near Barbados, since there were no more radio messages after March 5.

The heavy winds off the southern U.S. coast were unnoticed and forgotten but they may have overturned the *Cyclops* in seconds.

But a question still remains. Why didn't the ship break radio silence after March 5, if it was within miles of Norfolk? Could the radio have been damaged?

Until the underwater wreck is definitely identified as the *Cyclops*, the reason for her disappearance will still be an unsolved mystery.

The Red Baron

❧ 1940 ❧

In 1940, during World War II, the German Luftwaffe (air force) sent endless numbers of planes across the English Channel from occupied France to bomb London. It was called the *"blitzkrieg"* (lightning war). Night after night, the Germans dropped their bombs over the British city.

But the English never gave up! They survived the death and destruction. With the help of America's entrance into the war in 1941, they went on to victory over the Nazis.

During the blitz, a young RAF (Royal Air Force) fighter pilot was on his first night patrol over English shores. His name was Grayson.

The weather was clear in some areas and cloudy in others. The water in the channel below was choppy and the wind blew off and on, scattering the clouds.

It was a gloomy night and Grayson felt totally alone. Suddenly out of the clouds, he saw what appeared to be a single airplane.

"A German plane," he thought to himself and speeded up to catch it. The other plane swung away, heading across the channel towards France.

"Oh no you don't, Adolph," said Grayson, who increased his speed.

Suddenly, the enemy plane flew into the clear and, in the moonlight, Grayson saw that the aircraft was marked with black crosses.

"Definitely German markings," thought Grayson. "But wait a minute." He shook his head, not believing what he saw. "This couldn't be a Luftwaffe plane. It looks like something from the history books."

The plane was dark red, had three wings, each on top of the other. "It's a triplane from the first war," he thought in shock, "and it's flying faster than I am. That's impossible!"

Grayson rubbed his eyes. "Nobody will believe this," he thought. When he looked again, it was raining and difficult to see. Seconds later, the cloudburst ended, but the strange plane had disappeared.

"I must have been imagining all this," he said out loud. "Could I have dozed off for a moment and dreamed it?" Grayson shrugged it off, turned back, and completed his patrol.

Later, on the ground, after a few drinks with the other pilots, Grayson told the story of what had happened. "Incredible, isn't it?" he laughed. But everyone in the room was strangely quiet. You could hear a pin drop.

"What is it?" he asked. "Did I say the wrong thing?"

Finally, one of the older, veteran pilots spoke

up. "Nothing's wrong, lad. You finally met the Red Baron, that's all. Some call him the Red Knight."

"Who is he?" Grayson questioned.

"He's the ghost of Baron von Richthofen," explained the pilot, "the number one German fighter pilot of World War I. He was killed in 1918, though they don't know exactly how it happened."

"My own father flew against the Baron over twenty years ago," declared another pilot. "We've all seen him. Welcome to the club, Grayson."

They raised their glasses. "A toast to the Red Baron!"

Grayson gulped down his drink. "Dead now for twenty-two years," he thought to himself.

When the war ended in 1945, the Red Baron was never seen again.

Mermaid and Friends

❧ 1829 ❧

Luck is a mysterious force that either brings good fortune and happiness, or misfortune and tragedy. Just like people, ships have good luck or bad luck.

"Abandon ship!" yelled Captain Samuel Nolbrow. "We're breaking up!" The schooner *Mermaid* had crashed into an underwater coral reef. Bound for Hong Kong, she sailed out of Sydney, Australia with twenty-one people aboard.

It was 1829 and the *Mermaid* was going down fast in the Torres Strait between Australia and New Guinea. The crew and passengers managed to grab onto rocks and waited to be rescued.

Some time later the three-masted vessel, *Swiftsure*, sailed through the strait and picked up the exhausted survivors of the *Mermaid*.

Their joy was short-lived, however. The *Swiftsure* ran aground two days later and broke up on the rocks. The fourteen crew members and twenty-one survivors of the *Mermaid* all swam ashore.

The thirty-five people, alone on the rocky beach, wondered if they would ever be rescued. But their luck held when a ship called the *Governor Ready* happened by.

"We're headed for New Guinea," explained the captain. "Welcome aboard."

The *Governor Ready*'s thirty-two-man crew made the others comfortable with food, drink, and blankets. They were happy and contented . . . but not for long.

A fire broke out on the ship and everyone escaped in the lifeboats. Now sixty-seven survivors from three different ships waited for rescue.

After a time, the *Comet*, with a crew of twenty-one, sailed by and picked up all sixty-seven. Before they could get comfortable, a terrible storm struck. Gale force winds, a driving rain, and pounding waves caused the ship to sink. The familiar cry of "Abandon Ship!" rang out again.

But along came the *Jupiter*. Her crew of thirty-eight rescued all the survivors. Before they had a chance to dry off, the *Jupiter* went aground on a coral reef which tore a hole in her bottom.

One hundred twenty-six people escaped death by grabbing onto rocks along the reef. Soon, the *City of Leeds* sailed by and rescued everyone. Along with her one hundred passengers and crew the *City of Leeds* sailed into New Guinea safely!

Whether the survivors of this ordeal ever set foot in a sailing ship again after their incredible experience is not known. However, not one person from the *Mermaid, Swiftsure, Governor Ready, Comet,* or *Jupiter* lost his or her life. That mysterious force of good luck smiled on them all in the end.

But the ships weren't so lucky. All were lost, the victims of a string of unexplained bad luck.

Joyita

❧ 1955 ❧

"*Joyita* found half-waterlogged ... nobody on board ... no logbook or message found ..."

This radio message was sent in November 1955 by Captain Gerald Douglas of the British ship, *Tuvalu*. The *Joyita* had been missing for five weeks and now all twenty-five people on board had vanished.

For years she was called "the jinx ship" and "a bad luck boat." After her last voyage, many referred to her as the "*Mary Celeste* of the Pacific."

The story of the *Joyita* (which means "little jewel" in Spanish) begins in Los Angeles where she was built in 1931. Her first owners were a movie director and actress.

The seventy-ton *Joyita* was sixty-nine feet long and very luxurious. Her passengers were mainly movie stars. An actress named Thelma Todd died mysteriously in 1935 and some say it happened on board the *Joyita*.

After that, the boat had several owners. In 1941

the U.S. Navy used her as a patrol boat. She was taken to Pearl Harbor on December 6, the day before the Japanese attack on American ships. At that time, a watchman was found dead in her engine room. He had inhaled fumes from leaking battery acid.

After the war, the *Joyita* was changed to a fishing boat. She was fitted with a refrigerated hold, new engines, and 640 cubic feet of cork in her hull. The cork made her "unsinkable."

In 1952 the boat was sold to Dr. Ellen Luomala who rented it to her friend, Captain Thomas "Dusty" Miller. Miller tried to make a living with the *Joyita* as a fishing boat first in Hawaii and then Samoa in the Fiji Islands of the South Pacific. But the bad luck continued. Her engines broke down. Once she collided with another boat. Then she ran aground. Later, the *Joyita* caught fire. A crewman was even lost overboard.

The *Joyita*'s reputation as a jinx ship spread throughout Samoa. By 1955, Dusty Miller had no money and was deeply in debt. Although he was a well-liked and popular man, Miller had trouble finding anyone to work aboard her.

Things looked grim for Miller until he got a job delivering food and other supplies to the Tokelau Islands. On the return trip, Miller would load the *Joyita* with eighty tons of copra (dried coconut meat), which was the Islands' only product.

Captain Miller worked hard to get the *Joyita* seaworthy for the voyage but she was in poor condition. He managed to find a crew at the last moment. Though she wasn't supposed to carry paying passengers, Miller took on twenty-five people, including a woman and two children.

For some unexplained reason, Miller filled up the *Joyita*'s fuel tanks with enough gas for a three-thousand-mile journey. But his trip to the Tokelau Islands and back was only about five hundred miles. There was also enough food and water to last three weeks, much more than what was needed for the six days he'd be away. Why so much fuel and supplies? What Captain Miller had in mind will never be known.

There were many questions about the condition of the *Joyita*'s engine and radio equipment. In his rush to begin the journey and finally get a paying job, Captain Miller may have overlooked certain problems or been careless.

Miller never tested the radio before leaving. He never contacted the radio station in Apia, West Samoa, as he was asked to do by officials. Once the *Joyita* left Apia, she was never heard from again.

The *Joyita* set out on October 2, and before she could clear the harbor her engine broke down. The crew worked all night making repairs and the *Joyita* finally sailed away at 5:00 A.M. on the morning of October 3. Some believed that Miller knew he would be stopped by officials if he left later in the morning.

Weeks later, after Captain Douglas discovered the *Joyita* drifting and deserted, there were many unanswered questions about her last voyage. First and most important, what happened to the crew and passengers?

The *Joyita* had no lifeboat. It carried life jackets

and only three small rafts and these were missing. Why would the people have left the unsinkable *Joyita*, which was waterlogged but still afloat, to take their chances on rafts in shark-infested waters? And if they did, and overturned, where were the remains of the bodies and the debris from the rafts?

Based on the number of gallons of fuel still left in her tanks, it's believed that what happened to the *Joyita* occurred on the first night out. It was later found that there was a break in the radio transmitter antenna so no SOS signals could have been heard.

The cargo of the *Joyita* disappeared with the people including lumber, empty oil drums, and heavy sacks of rice, sugar, and flour. Was the cargo stolen by pirates and the crew and passengers murdered? Was everything tossed overboard to lighten the ship? But there was no sign of any of the cargo in the surrounding area.

It was discovered that a rusted pipe in the engine room had caused flooding. Because the leak was hidden under the engine floor, it went unnoticed until it was too late. The *Joyita* was flooded, with no power or radio, adrift in the ocean.

Did the passengers panic and leave the boat thinking it was sinking? Why didn't Captain Miller reassure them the *Joyita* wouldn't sink because of the cork in the hull?

Some believe that Miller was injured and possibly dead and couldn't communicate at all. Medical instruments and bloodstained bandages were found on board. The captain or someone else may have been the victim of an accident or fight. If the panicked crew and passengers abandoned the *Joyita* using the rafts, how did the cargo disappear? Did looters arrive later and take it?

There are other theories. One newspaper reported that some Japanese from a nearby fishing fleet murdered the people and took the cargo. They did this because those aboard the *Joyita* had seen something they shouldn't have.

A Russian submarine is said to have taken the cargo and passengers so her position wouldn't be revealed. But this is unlikely since submarines don't have much space for extra people and supplies.

Japanese soldiers left over from World War II, hiding on deserted islands in the Pacific, may have turned pirate and captured them all. No one really knows, but it *is* true that during the 1950s forty Japanese soldiers in hiding were discovered on such islands. (The war ended in 1945.)

There are other facts about the *Joyita* which add confusion to the mystery. The steering gear didn't work and the rudder was jammed. Part of the boat's structure was missing, including the funnel. All these things pointed to a collision at sea. Did another vessel ram the drifting *Joyita* and rescue the passengers? If so, why weren't they heard from? Or was it just the heavy battering of powerful waves which caused the damage?

Someone had rigged a piece of canvas above the forward cabin. Was it an awning for the sun or used for catching rain for drinking water? Did several of the crew remain on board after the other passengers abandoned the *Joyita*? If so, what happened to them? Were they murdered or taken prisoner by pirates, looters, Japanese soldiers, or Russians?

There are many questions, but few answers to the mystery of the *Joyita*.

The famous "jinx ship" was sold at auction and, in 1957, she ran aground on a reef. Since then, she has been sold to many owners for smaller amounts of money.

Most of the islanders wanted nothing to do with the *Joyita*. Many said she was haunted and the voices of the missing passengers could still be heard in her hull.

One owner wanted to fix up the *Joyita* and turn her into an attraction for tourists. The locals didn't mind working on deck or outside the ship, but they refused to go below. So the *Joyita* was left on a beach rusting and rotting in the sun.

DC-3

It's likely that the passengers on board the DC-3 airplane bound for Miami were a happy group.

"We wish you a Merry Christmas and a Happy New Year . . ." they may have sung since they were flying home from San Juan, Puerto Rico, after a short Christmas holiday.

"Oh come, all ye faithful, joyful and triumphant . . ." chanted the twenty-seven passengers on board. Christmas may have been over for three days that December 28, 1948, but the holiday spirit was still alive and well on the plane.

The chartered flight had left the airport in San Juan at 10:03 that night. It was expected to arrive in Miami at about four o'clock in the early morning hours.

It had been a long night for pilot Robert Linquist and copilot Ernest Hill. The two had flown in from Miami at 7:40 that evening.

Captain Linquist reported that the landing gear warning lights weren't working right. Repair crews found that the plane's batteries needed re-charging and the water level in the batteries was low. Since it would have taken a few hours to re-charge the batteries, Linquist had the repair crew just add water and return them to the plane without charging.

More battery trouble was reported later and the flight was delayed. Apparently, the plane's receiver and transmitter were working irregularly. They had no radio contact with the tower but CAA Communications at San Juan was able to pick up their messages.

Since the DC-3 was in otherwise good working order, it left for Miami and advised CAA Communications it was on its way. Later in the flight, the Overseas Foreign Air Route Traffic Control Center at Miami received a message: "We're at 8,500 feet and our ETA (estimated time of arrival) in Miami is 0400 hours."

Much later, the Air Traffic Control in New Orleans picked up another message from the DC-3: "We're fifty miles south of Miami and standing by for landing instructions. Over."

This was the last contact anyone ever had with the airplane. San Juan, Miami, and New Orleans all tried to contact the flight but couldn't.

"This is Miami Control. Be advised that there is a change in wind direction from northwest to northeast. Please correct your approach and give us your position. Over, do you read?" It's not known if the DC-3 ever received this information from the tower at Miami.

After the flight was long overdue, the U.S. Coast Guard was notified and a search began. The DC-3 had disappeared, only minutes away from its destination. No one in the area had seen or heard anything unusual.

The weather was perfect on the day of the search. The sea was calm. The water was so clear in the shallow area south of Miami that a large object, such as the body of an airplane, could easily be spotted.

If the plane went down in the Florida Keys, it would be found. Any wreckage, bodies, oil slicks, or debris from the missing aircraft would be seen.

But not a single trace of the DC-3 or its crew and passengers was ever found. It totally vanished.

The Civil Aeronautics Board (CAB) report on the incident mentioned that the plane had some difficulty with its electrical system. This affected some lights and the radio's transmitter and receiver.

If the electrical trouble also affected the plane's automatic compass, Captain Linquist may not have known the real location of the DC-3. Perhaps he wasn't fifty miles south of Miami as he reported in his last radio message. He may have been much farther away.

The CAB report also stated that the DC-3 had 7½ hours worth of fuel. The last message from the plane was 6 hours and 10 minutes into the flight. There was only 1 hour and 20 minutes worth of fuel left.

If Captain Linquist never received the information about the change in wind direction, the plane could have unknowingly drifted off course. Instead of heading into Miami, the DC-3 might have drifted over the Gulf of Mexico.

Linquist may have repeatedly tried to signal for help when he saw the plane was rapidly running out of fuel. But the radio wasn't working properly and no one heard the call. The plane might have plunged into the Gulf, its wreckage carried away by the Gulf Stream current forever.

There are others who believe the DC-3 was spirited away by a mysterious force, possibly not of this earth. Some think it may have entered another dimension of place and time.

But the actual cause of the plane's disappearance will never be known for sure. It will always remain a mystery.

Bavaria

❧ 1889 ❧

There was a storm and now a ship was missing at the eastern end of Lake Ontario. (Ontario is one of the five Great Lakes between Canada and the United States.)

It was May 1889, and the *Armenia* was one of several rescue vessels sent out to search for the lost *Bavaria*.

"Up ahead, Captain. She's aground on Galloo Island," shouted one of the crewmen.

There was the *Bavaria* stuck tight on a small shallow sandbar. When they were closer, the crew called out, but no one answered. The ship was eerily silent.

The *Armenia*'s captain led a boarding party to search the apparently deserted vessel.

"There's some water in her hold, Captain," said the first mate, "but otherwise, she's fit to sail."

"And not a trace of the crew," remarked the skipper.

All important papers and a large amount of money lay untouched in the captain's quarters.

"Look here in the galley (kitchen)," shouted one of the crew. "Some freshly baked bread."

They found tools on the deck where a seaman had been doing some repair work. "It looks like the sailor was right in the middle of a job but never came back to finish," said the first mate.

"And her lifeboat is missing," the captain stated. "They must have left in a hurry."

"I found this in one of the cabins, skipper." The crewman held up a chirping canary in a cage.

"It appears that this bird is the only thing living on this ship," declared the mate.

The *Armenia* sailed back to port to report the news of the *Bavaria*. Many expected members of the crew to turn up later and explain the mystery. But no one ever did and bodies were never found.

All evidence pointed to the fact that the crew abandoned the ship quickly and unexpectedly. But what made them leave so fast? There was nothing wrong with the *Bavaria*. And what happened to the crew?

Some believe the storm made the crew think the ship might turn over. But what about the repair job and the baking of fresh bread? These were not things crewmen would do during a terrible storm. They were normal, everyday tasks. Something must have happened to cause all on board to leave.

Days later, the captain of another ship claimed his crew had seen two men in a lifeboat on the lake. But they couldn't reach the boat and it disappeared in a thick fog. The strange thing was that the men sat completely still and made no effort to help in their own rescue.

A lighthouse keeper reported a similar incident about two men in a lifeboat.

Some claim that something monstrous and unnatural threatened the *Bavaria*. All aboard became insane and tried to escape or kill themselves. Whatever made them flee from the ship ended up causing their apparent deaths.

What happened to the crew of the *Bavaria* remains a mystery.

Sao Paulo

❧ 1951 ❧

MISSING: ONE TWENTY-THOUSAND-TON BATTLESHIP. LAST SEEN IN THE NORTH ATLANTIC, SOMEWHERE OFF THE AZORES, WITH EIGHT CREWMEN ABOARD.

The disappearance of the battleship, *Sao Paulo*, took place in 1951. Built in 1910 for the Brazilian Navy, she was five hundred feet long with three continuous decks. Her sides were armor plated and she carried thirty mounted guns. The *Sao Paulo* was retired in 1946, left alone and forgotten.

In 1951 the British Iron and Steel Corporation, a salvage company, paid to have the *Sao Paulo* towed to Britain. There they would break her up and use the scrap metal.

Two tugs, the *Bustler* and the *Dexterous*, were to tow her across the Atlantic. A crew of eight from Scotland were responsible for making her safe enough for the voyage.

All openings were closed securely so seawater wouldn't get in. All guns were fixed in place. The

ship was made totally watertight for its last voyage. It needed to be stable in the water since there might be bad weather during the trip.

After the work was completed and thoroughly inspected, the Brazilian officials gave the *Sao Paulo* a "certificate of seaworthiness."

Two lifeboats and life jackets were stowed on the battleship. The crew of eight would stay aboard the *Sao Paulo* while she was being towed and keep order.

A portable radio was put aboard, as well as lights to be used at night to alert passing vessels of a ship in tow.

The trip began on September 20, 1951. The two tugs had more than enough power to get the job done. The battleship was attached to the tugs by two long towlines.

They moved slowly but steadily along. Twice, the *Sao Paulo* seemed to list (tilt) but it was corrected both times.

By early November, they were near the Azores when gale force winds brought them to a complete stop. The tugs and battleship rolled and pitched in the water. The rain increased. Water was blowing everywhere but all three ships remained stable.

But at dawn, the storm got worse. Walls of water threatened the ships.

"We've got a problem back there," screamed one of the crewmen on the *Bustler* over the sound of the wind.

The *Sao Paulo* was swinging wildly in the sea. She moved up and down violently, suddenly turning and rolling.

"Tighten the towlines," shouted crewmen on the tugs who tried unsuccessfully to control the huge battleship.

"She's pulling us back with her," the men yelled as the two tugs were forced together helplessly.

"Give me full power." Both tugs tried to pull away from each other. The *Bustler* and *Dexterous* were within a few feet of crashing into each other.

"Slip the towline," the captain of the *Dexterous* shouted to the chief engineer. At that moment, the *Bustler*'s towline broke away, too.

The storm was so bad that both tugs did all they could just to keep their position. The wind was shrieking. Water crashed over them and it became dark.

Neither tug could reach the crew of the *Sao Paulo* after flashing signal lights or by radio.

"She doesn't show on the radar screen, Captain," said the worried radarman. "It's like she disappeared instantly."

"How can that be possible?" asked the captain.

After a time, the storm passed and the tugs searched for days looking for any trace of the *Sao Paulo*. No boats, bodies, or even a life jacket was ever found even after a week-long search by other ships and airplanes. Day and night radar watches were kept in case the battleship had drifted away during the storm.

After a full investigation by the British Ministry of Transport, it was concluded that the *Sao Paulo* probably sank while out of control. Heavy rolling occurred and large amounts of water may have entered the hull (body of the ship).

Two ships later reported seeing mysterious

flashing lights that night, after the towlines broke. But one sighting was 230 miles away and the other was 160 miles away.

The twenty-thousand-ton battleship, *Sao Paulo*, disappeared without a trace. According to author Alan Villiers, it was "as if some mighty force had plucked at those broken towlines and dragged her, in an instant, down beneath the sea."

Blimp L-18

❧ 1942 ❧

"Oil slick below," reported Ensign Adams. He pointed down into the waters of San Francisco Bay.

"Let's take a closer look," said Lieutenant Cody who radioed the information back to the naval base. "It could be an enemy sub."

Blimp L-18 was on a routine patrol one morning in 1942. After the Japanese attack on Pearl Harbor the previous year, the United States was afraid that enemy submarines would try to attack the West Coast.

Ships from the Pacific Fleet were anchored in the bay. Large helium-filled blimps were used to guard and patrol the area. They were powered by airplane engines and carried depth charges (underwater bombs). If an enemy sub was spotted, the blimp could float above the water and drop the depth charges on the submerged sub.

Two fishing boats and their crews watched from

a distance as the blimp came down slowly. Two armed patrol boats had also been alerted.

The blimp floated above the oil slick. But instead of dropping a depth charge, it lifted up quickly and disappeared in the clouds.

A few hours later, some fishermen on the beach glanced up to see a blimp traveling slowly toward them. It touched down and they ran to grab it. But the large balloon dragged them along the shore. As it started to lift off, the fishermen looked inside the compartment (gondola) where the pilot and co-pilot sat. What they saw made them stand up straight and scratch their heads.

There was no one aboard the blimp! The L-18 was flying by itself. But where were Lieutenant Cody and Ensign Adams? How could they have disappeared?

As it rose upward, the balloon bumped against a jagged cliff near the beach. One of the huge depth charges came loose and fell, unexploded, to the ground. Now three hundred pounds lighter, the blimp shot up into the sky and disappeared from view. Sometime later, the L-18 drifted down in a crumbled heap onto the streets of Daly City, a small town outside of San Francisco.

Residents of the area immediately contacted the Navy about the strange pilotless blimp. A salvage crew went to the neighborhood and took the L-18 back to the base.

After a Navy investigation, the blimp was found to be undamaged. Everything was in place where it was supposed to be. The life raft and parachutes were still in the gondola.

How did the two crewmen vanish from the

blimp? Did they fall overboard into the ocean when they were checking out the oil slick? Were they still inside the gondola when the blimp suddenly shot up above the slick? Or was that the moment the men disappeared and the blimp lifted suddenly because it was a few hundred pounds lighter?

Not one person on the fishing boats or Navy patrol vessels saw anyone fall in the water. The two airmen were wearing bright yellow life jackets. Surely, someone would have seen the yellow jackets and the splash in the water.

But no bodies or life jackets were ever found. The two men apparently vanished without a trace. But to where did they vanish? Did they disappear in time? Were they snatched away by a mysterious force? What happened to them?

Witchcraft

❧ 1967 ❧

"If you don't have any plans tonight, Father, how about joining me on my boat, *Witchcraft*?" asked Daniel Burack, a retired hotel manager. "I'll take her a mile or so out and we can see the Christmas lights of the city."

"Sounds wonderful, Dan. I could use some rest and relaxation," replied his friend, Reverend Father Patrick Horgan.

On the evening of December 22, 1967, the two men were aboard Burack's twenty-three-foot cabin cruiser, *Witchcraft*. From a mile out in the ocean, they were able to see the entire city of Miami Beach with its multicolored holiday lights. It was a beautiful sight and the two friends talked and enjoyed the view.

The sea wasn't as calm as Burack had hoped and northerly winds were making the water somewhat rough and choppy. As the *Witchcraft* made its way back to port, Burack, an expert sailor and navigator, heard a strange sound. Then the engine started to vibrate loudly.

"I'm shutting it down, Father," he explained. "I think the propeller hit something underwater. I'll radio the Coast Guard for a tow back to port." Burack added, "They should be here in a few minutes."

"We're so close to shore, Dan," said Father Horgan, "maybe we should just swim in?" Both men laughed.

The Coast Guard Office in Miami received a call from the *Witchcraft* at 9:00 P.M. Burack explained that the hull was not damaged and they were in no danger. But the *Witchcraft* was disabled and they'd need a tow home.

The cruiser had foam flotation chambers which were supposed to make it "unsinkable." There were also flares and life preservers on board.

Burack said the *Witchcraft* was near Buoy Number 7 (a floating marker in the water). The Coast Guard asked Burack to fire a flare in fifteen to twenty minutes to guide them to his location.

In the meantime, Burack and Father Horgan enjoyed some refreshment and waited for the tow. Nineteen minutes later, the Coast Guard arrived in the area, but there was no sign of the *Witchcraft* or the two men. No flare had been fired. No other radio messages were received.

After a five-day search by the Civil Air Patrol, the Coast Guard, and private boats and planes, not a single clue turned up as to their disappearance. The search covered an area of about twenty-five thousand square miles.

Some say the choppy seas flooded the boat. If

she was hit broadside by a large wave, she could have overturned. But Burack was an experienced sailor. Knowing help was on the way, he could have used the engine (which was vibrating but not dead) to keep the *Witchcraft* headed into the waves and afloat.

The cruiser was supposed to be unsinkable. If the boat was flooded, she wasn't supposed to plunge to the bottom. The condition of the sea that night listed waves at four to six feet. Could waves that size totally swamp the *Witchcraft*? If it was overwhelmed, why wasn't there any wreckage or debris found on the surface? And where were the bodies of Burack and Father Horgan?

Why didn't Burack use the radio if he felt the *Witchcraft* was in danger? Or did something happen so fast that there was no time to radio for help?

One moment, the two were relaxing on the boat, watching the lights of Miami only a mile away. The next moment, they had vanished along with a twenty-three-foot cabin cruiser.

The boat lived up to her name. Perhaps it was *Witchcraft*.

P-51 Mustang

❧ 1948 ❧

"You say you saw a huge disc in the sky?" asked the commanding officer of Godman Field outside Fort Knox in Kentucky. "And it's headed this way?"

The officer held back a chuckle. He was talking to a state policeman and the story was difficult to believe.

"You say some Army MPs (military police) also saw this object?" He thought to himself, "Maybe there's something to this after all."

Out loud he said, "We appreciate your notifying us, Captain, and we will be on ready alert status until this matter is cleared up."

The police hadn't been imagining things that January 7, 1948. Thirty minutes later, a huge, shiny disc appeared over the base. It floated motionless near some clouds. Witnesses saw a strange red glow coming from it, that seemed to brighten and dim continuously.

Captain Thomas Mantell was ordered to inves-

tigate the object. He and two other pilots took off in their P-51 Mustangs to get a closer look.

Mantell was in the lead plane, far ahead of the other two. He radioed back to base. "It's directly ahead of me, moving at about half my speed. The thing looks metallic and is of tremendous size."

As Mantell climbed toward it in the Mustang, the object started to climb too, and picked up speed.

"It's still above me, making my speed or better," he reported. "I'm going to twenty thousand feet. If I'm no closer, I'll abandon chase."

Those were the last words ever spoken by Thomas Mantell. Seconds later, witnesses saw the P-51 Mustang break apart in midair as though some powerful hammer had smashed it to pieces.

The parts of the airplane, many of them small fragments, scattered over a large area on the ground. There had been no explosion and no fire. The strange disc had disappeared from sight.

The wreckage was collected and the Air Force began an investigation that lasted for two years. Their official findings were that Captain Mantell was chasing Venus, the second planet from the sun, which was often visible in the sky. He blacked out when he flew too high without oxygen and the Mustang crashed in the power dive that happened after the blackout.

However, the Air Force didn't say that Venus was barely visible that day. It was only a pinpoint of light in the sky. Also, Mantell described the object as "tremendous in size."

In 1951 the Air Force revealed that what Mantell saw that afternoon wasn't Venus after all. It was a large weather balloon which, in 1948, was a military secret called "Project Skyhook." The balloon traveled an average of 175 miles per hour, sometimes looked metallic in the sunlight, and could inflate up to one hundred feet in diameter.

Was an experienced pilot like Captain Mantell actually chasing a giant weather balloon? Another P-51 continued searching the area minutes after the Mantell incident, but found nothing. Could a balloon have disappeared from sight so quickly?

What caused the airplane to break apart into small pieces suddenly in midair, as some witnesses said? Or did it crash after a power dive when Captain Mantell blacked out?

The Air Force believed it solved the mystery of the P-51, but others are still doubtful. What do you think?

Carroll A. Deering

❧ 1921 ❦

It was one of the last five-masted trading ships. The 2,110-ton *Carroll A. Deering* was built in 1919 and named after the son of the shipbuilder.

In 1920 the *Deering* left for Rio de Janeiro, Brazil from Maine with a cargo of coal. Her captain became ill, and he left the ship accompanied by his son, the first mate.

The new captain was sixty-six-year-old Willis Wormell, an experienced seaman, but recently retired. The new mate was Charles McLellan, supposedly a heavy drinker and troublemaker.

The *Deering* arrived in Rio and unloaded the cargo. Then she started back for Norfolk, Virginia with a stop in Barbados.

Prohibition (no liquor) was the law in the United States and rum was available everywhere in Barbados and other parts of the West Indies. During the stopover, the crew of the *Deering* drank heavily and the first mate, McLellan, ended up in jail.

Captain Wormell managed to get the crew back

on board and have McLellan released. Then the *Deering* set sail for Norfolk. It was January 9, 1921.

After a vicious storm and gale force winds, the five-master was spotted by another ship off the coast of North Carolina. But things were not right. The crew was gathered on the quarterdeck, something the captain would never have allowed. (The quarterdeck is reserved for officers.)

One of the crew shouted through a megaphone, "We've lost two anchors. Report it ashore." These may have been the last words from any member of the crew of the *Deering*.

The passing ship's radio was out so it tried to relay the *Deering*'s message to a nearby steamer. This unidentified steamer didn't stop and it was never seen again. Some believe it was the *Hewitt*, which disappeared later in the same area.

Two days later, the *Carroll A. Deering* was discovered aground on the Diamond Shoals, off the North Carolina coast. All sails were set and she was abandoned—not a trace of the twelve-man crew or captain.

After a search of the deserted vessel, it was found that the *Deering*'s steering equipment was smashed. A sledgehammer lay nearby. All personal belongings were missing, including Captain Wormell's own gear. The papers, logbook, and compass were also gone.

Yet the *Deering* was undamaged and fairly close to shore. The captain's handwriting marked the ship's course on a chart found on board. Then a different handwriting took over. It also appeared as though several people had been sleeping in the captain's cabin.

Food was still in the galley and dinner was being prepared when the ship was abandoned. Two of the lifeboats were missing. The only thing left on board were two cats, which were saved and given new homes.

Many people have tried to explain the mystery of the *Carroll A. Deering*.

Some believe the crew thought the ship was in danger during the storm and became panic-stricken. They attempted to reach shore in the lifeboats and never made it. Or perhaps, they were picked up by the passing steamer, the *Hewitt*, which also disappeared. No wreckage or bodies were ever found.

Many people believed the crew and captain were victims of pirates or Russian kidnappers who imprisoned the crew and took them away to Russia. But why take the crew and leave the ship, without trying to free her from the Diamond Shoals? The *Deering* was carrying no cargo and she might have been freed by using her backup engine.

Others believe it was mutiny. The crew, led by McLellan, killed the captain. That's why they had assembled on the quarterdeck and why someone else took over for the captain, writing up the *Deering*'s position on the ship's chart.

Were they working with rumrunners from the *Hewitt*, trying to use the *Deering* to smuggle liquor into the United States? Did they abandon the *Deering* after it ran aground and then become lost in the lifeboats or on the *Hewitt*?

Which was it—murder, mutiny, piracy, storms,

kidnapping, rumrunners, or Russians—and not a trace of the crew or any wreckage?

What really happened to the crew of the *Deering* remains a big question mark.

But it *is* known what happened to the ship itself. The five-master settled deeply into the Diamond Shoals sandbar. Anything of value on her was taken away for salvage.

Several weeks later, the *Deering* was dynamited. The bow (front) washed ashore in 1922. More than thirty years later, it was swept back to sea by a hurricane.

Small pieces of the *Deering* are sometimes carried onto the beach and sold in local shops as souvenirs. The bell and lights were returned to Maine and kept by Carroll A. Deering, the man for whom the ship was named.

Flight 401

❧ 1972 ❧

A stewardess at Eastern Air Lines, on a flight from New York to Florida, suddenly saw something in her mind that made her sit down. She clearly saw a large jet approaching Miami and flying over the Everglades. It was late at night. She saw the wing crumble and the jet crash into the ground. She could actually hear the passengers cry for help.

Shaken up, the stewardess told her friends, two other flight attendants. "It'll happen around the holidays. It won't be us," she whispered. "But it *will* be real close." After a time, the frightening vision faded from her mind and memory.

On Friday, December 29, 1972, Flight 401 was scheduled to leave Kennedy Airport in New York at 9:00 P.M. It was one of Eastern Air Lines' brand-new wide-body jumbo jets, the L-1011. They cost more than $15 million each and could carry over 250 passengers. They were called "Whisperliners" because the planes were so quiet, clean, and inviting.

The crew in the cockpit were all experienced airmen—Captain Bob Loft, First Officer Albert Stockstill, and Second Officer Don Repo.

In a last-minute switch, the stewardess who had the strange vision two weeks before, and her two friends were part of the team of attendants assigned to Flight 401. The crew which was supposed to work 401, was arriving late from another flight.

Twenty minutes before the scheduled departure time, the regular cabin crew finally arrived to take over from the substitutes. The stewardess who had the vision went back to her original flight. It was close, but she and her friends didn't have to work Flight 401 that night.

There were 163 passengers and thirteen crew members on board the big L-1011. The plane was in the air by 9:20 P.M. and heading south to Miami. The flight was smooth and hours later, the Whisperliner started its descent pattern as it approached the Miami airport. The landing gear and wheels were lowered into place beneath the airplane.

"Only two of the three landing gear lights are on," said Captain Loft.

"There's no nose gear," stated the copilot.

The plane couldn't land safely until the problem was solved. "We'll have to circle for a while," the captain explained to the tower.

Either the forward gear which lowered the wheels was stuck, or the light that signaled the gear was down and in position was burned out.

The cockpit crew had to find out what was going on before the plane could attempt a landing.

First they decided to try to change the gear light. The plane was put on automatic pilot, holding it at an altitude of two thousand feet. When Loft leaned across to try to get to the light, the pressure on the control column apparently disconnected the automatic pilot. His indicator light (which showed how high the plane was) went off. But copilot Stockstill's autopilot didn't go off. His altitude indicator light was still on so Stockstill thought the plane was on automatic pilot at the correct altitude. Neither Loft nor Stockstill could see each other's altitude indicator.

Stockstill couldn't get the tiny light out. Captain Loft also tried but it was jammed in tight. Then Loft ordered Officer Repo down into the nose-wheel well to try to see firsthand if the nose gear was down and locked.

Flight 401 was now crossing the black swampland of the Everglades near Miami. It was at two thousand feet but started to drop slowly in altitude when the autopilot was disconnected. Loft and Stockstill were still trying to loosen the light.

As the plane dropped to seventeen hundred feet, a chime sounded near Officer Repo's panel. It warned the crew of a drop in altitude. But Repo was below checking out the nose gear. There was no light down there and he couldn't see very well. No one heard the chime above the noise in the cockpit. Stockstill was keeping track of the flight but his autopilot said the plane was still at two thousand feet.

The controller at the Miami airport noticed that

Flight 401 had dropped in altitude to nine hundred feet. But he was busy with six other planes approaching and taking off from the airport.

No one in the cockpit could tell the plane had lost altitude. Below them, the Everglades were totally black. The autopilot still read two thousand feet.

It was 11:42 P.M. The L-1011 was at six hundred feet and falling. Stockstill turned to Loft and asked, "We're still at two thousand, right?"

Then Loft yelled, "What's happening here?"

At that moment, Flight 401 disappeared from the radar screen.

Other planes contacted the tower, "We saw a big explosion. There was a large orange flash." Flight 401 had crashed in the Everglades!

The plane broke into pieces on impact. Bodies and debris were everywhere. Ninety-nine people lost their lives, including all three members of the flight crew—Loft, Repo, and Stockstill. Seventy-seven miraculously survived the crash.

The stewardess who had the vision about a crash over the Everglades heard about the accident when she stepped off her assigned flight in Fort Lauderdale, Florida. She might have been on 401 if the original crew hadn't come on at the last minute.

She said to her friends, "I knew it was going to be close." They all remembered.

"It might have been us," they thought.

After a thorough investigation it was decided that the crew didn't monitor the flight instruments during the last few minutes of the flight. The drop in altitude wasn't noticed until it was too late. The problem with the landing gear light drew the crew's total attention away from the other instruments and the different autopilot readings. Until this tragedy, few pilots were aware that a slight pressure on the control column would turn off the autopilot.

The National Transportation Safety Board recommended a light switch near the nose gear so it could be seen clearly and a flashing light, as well as a chime, warning the crew of any altitude change. These and other changes were made in all L-1011 aircraft, making them among the safest in the air.

Also, a new system for ground controllers which made sure planes were at safe altitudes was developed by the Federal Aviation Administration.

But this is not the end of the story. Strange rumors began to circulate among the staff of Eastern Air Lines. Many stewardesses and crew members admitted that they saw the apparent ghosts of Captain Loft and Officer Repo appear on other L-1011 flights.

In one instance, it was reported that Repo said clearly, "There will never be another crash of an L-1011. We will not let it happen."

The ghosts of Repo and Loft were thought to be protective of the planes. Many crew members believed that their appearance would guarantee a safe trip. Yet, there were others who were frightened and preferred not to work on the jumbo jets at all.

On one flight to Mexico City, Repo appeared in the galley and spoke clearly to the flight engineer and stewardesses. "Watch for fire on this airplane," and then he disappeared. Later, one of the engines stalled. The flight was cancelled and the engine had to be totally replaced.

Eastern Air Lines officials did not readily believe the stories about the ghosts of Repo and Loft. But since so many incidents were being reported, they took a more serious look. It seemed that there was a connection between the ghosts' appearances and planes that used spare parts from the wreckage of Flight 401. The ghosts appeared only on those planes that used parts from the crash!

The result was that mechanics were ordered to remove all parts from L-1011s which had originally been used on Flight 401, even if they were in perfect working order.

Reports of Loft stopped and only Repo seemed to be appearing in incidents. Some believed that Officer Repo was a disturbed soul who had difficulty accepting his sudden death. He needed help in moving on to the spiritual world.

Several seances were conducted where a small group of people tried to contact the dead. A number of flight personnel from the airline were involved in these seances as well as Repo's family members. He was contacted and urged to accept his death.

The incidents stopped and many believe that Don Repo's soul is now at rest. But now and then there are still stories about a mysterious ghost appearing on certain L-1011 aircraft.

Ourang Medan

❧ 1948 ❧

"Captain, we've received a Mayday from the Dutch freighter, *Ourang Medan*," said the worried radioman.

"Do you have her position?" asked the captain.

"Yes, sir. She's a few hours away," he replied, "in the Straits of Malacca between Malaya and Sumatra."

"All ahead full," ordered the captain who relayed the position of the freighter to the bridge.

A call for help from any ship in the area was top priority. The crew or passengers might be in danger and saving lives was another vessel's first responsibility.

"Captain, there's something you should know," said the radioman.

"What is it?" the captain asked.

"The freighter's radio operator said that the officers and crew were dead." He added, "His last words were, 'I die.' "

Sometime later, the *Ourang Medan* was sighted.

Smoke came from her funnel but she appeared to be drifting. No one was on deck and her radio was quiet.

The boarding parties found a shocking sight. Dead bodies were sprawled throughout the vessel. The radio operator was in his chair, one hand still on the transmitter. Even the ship's mascot, a dog, was dead.

The weather that day was clear and warm and the sea was calm when the grim discovery took place in 1948. One strange and terrible fact adds to the mystery. All of the faces of the dead were turned toward the sun. All eyes were open and staring. All mouths were open wide. Even the ship's dog died with its eyes open and teeth bared. Many say they all died in terror.

The boarding parties decided to tow what was now a death ship back to port. Whatever happened aboard the freighter needed to be investigated.

Suddenly, a fire erupted through one of the holds. Quickly the flames spread throughout the ship and out of control. Members of the boarding party ran for their lives back into the boats.

Minutes later, the *Ourang Medan* exploded in a burst of flame and smoke. Almost immediately, she sank into the deep waters of the Straits of Malacca. There hadn't even been time to make an accurate count of the number of dead on board. All evidence was lost forever.

What could have killed the entire crew (and the dog) so very quickly? Was it a rare infectious disease? But there is no virus in existence that could kill so fast. And diseases that affect humans don't always affect animals the same way.

Could it have been some type of poisoning? How could a poison be given to all members of the crew and the dog at the same time? Who would do such a thing and why?

Could gas leaks or fumes aboard ship have killed everyone? It's not likely in the open air on deck. People and animals die from gas or fumes with their eyes closed as though they were asleep. So why did all of the dead have that same terrified look on their faces?

There are more questions. Why did the fire break out right after the boarding parties arrived? Was the fire set to force them to leave the ship? Why did the explosion take place later as if it was purposely destroying all evidence?

If some unknown person, hiding on board, started the fire and then set off the explosion, that person would be dead, too! And if it wasn't a person, what was it?

Southern Cross Minor

❧ 1933 ❧

Bill Lancaster was going for the record—England to Cape Town, South Africa, in less than four days, six hours, and fifty-four minutes!

It was April 1933, and Lancaster's plane was a blue DeHavilland biplane with a 100-horsepower engine. He named it the *Southern Cross Minor*. (A biplane has two wings, one on top of the other.)

"Sleep will be out of the question for a few days," said the veteran aviator before takeoff.

Lancaster left Kent, England at 5:30 A.M. on April 11. He carried a package of chicken sandwiches and a chocolate bar, a two-gallon water tank, one flask of coffee, and another of water.

After refueling at Barcelona, Spain, Lancaster, fighting headwinds, landed at Oran, Algeria at 9:00 P.M. He was already 4½ hours behind the record and exhausted.

But he took off immediately and flew to Reggan, in the middle of the Sahara Desert. Strong winds and sandstorms delayed him even more and when

he landed at Reggan on the afternoon of the twelfth, he was totally worn-out.

To have a chance at the record, Lancaster had to take off immediately on a night flight across the Sahara in a blowing sandstorm. He had been in the air nearly thirty hours without rest.

The plane was refueled and Lancaster insisted he continue the flight.

"It's madness," said the French officials, who gave him matches and a flashlight.

"I'm going on," he replied.

Lancaster was so sleepy that he flew out of control for the first few minutes. Then he corrected himself and got back on course. Every so often, he'd look at his compass by shining the flashlight.

Ninety minutes later, at about 8:15 P.M., his engine misfired. Five minutes later, it missed again and the *Southern Cross Minor* began losing altitude.

Suddenly the engine cut off completely. "If I can glide to a landing," he thought to himself, "I can repair the damage."

It was hard to see the ground in the total blackness below the plane. The *Southern Cross Minor* hit the desert floor hard, splintered the propeller and bounced over on its back.

Lancaster was knocked unconscious. When he came to, he was bleeding from where his face had hit the instrument panel. The plane was damaged beyond repair but at least the drinking water was safe.

Lancaster decided to stay with the plane and wait to be rescued. He figured he was about twenty miles from the Trans-Saharan Road. Surely, the French would come looking for him.

He used his logbook as a diary and took the fabric from the plane to burn as flares during the night. He drank small amounts of his water regularly but the terrible heat of the day made him very thirsty. At night, it was so cold that he couldn't stop shivering.

The French had sent search vehicles (both planes and trucks) to look for the missing flyer. But they couldn't locate him and the days passed slowly and painfully for Lancaster.

By the sixth day, his face had swelled badly and he noticed his body skin had shrivelled. Flies kept buzzing around his head wounds and he was crazed with thirst. He was very weak now and could barely write.

On the seventh day, Bill Lancaster knew that this entry would be the final one in his diary. He drank the last of his water, knowing he would probably die the next day. Then he carefully wrapped the diary up in fabric and tied it with wire to the biplane.

Lancaster wanted his loved ones to read what he had written. It was the story of what happened and his last good-bye to them. On the morning of the twentieth, he wrote on a fuel card he carried, "So the beginning of the eighth day has dawned. It is still cool. I have no water. No wind. I am waiting patiently. Come soon, please. Fever racked me last night. Hope you get my full log. Bill."

Sometime that day, Bill Lancaster died, still waiting for his rescuers. They gave up the search and his disappearance in 1933 was an unsolved mystery.

Some said that Lancaster had purposely flown to his death because he couldn't break the flying record. Others believed he had been captured by Bedouin tribesmen in the desert.

Years passed. The French Army was involved in a war in Algeria. Patrols were sent all over the desert. In February 1962 some French soldiers were 150 miles south of Reggan, about 40 miles from the Trans-Saharan Road.

A small truck was driving over the desert.

"Look, sir, over there," the soldier pointed, "the wreck of a plane." They drove closer.

"It's a biplane," said the amazed soldier. "It must be twenty or thirty years old."

"Over here," yelled another. "A body . . . just sitting here."

Bill Lancaster's body had dried up in the hot desert sun and mummified. His features were still clear. The cuts on his head were there. His hand was grabbing at his throat.

The soldiers found the diary. Miraculously, the brittle pages were still intact. His story was finally told.

Lancaster was forty miles from the road. If he had left the plane and walked toward it, he could have been saved.

So the rescuers came after all . . . but they were twenty-nine years too late!

The Spray

❧ 1909 ❧

Captain Joshua Slocum and his sailboat, *The Spray*, made history in 1888. He became the first man to sail alone around the world. Slocum completed the three-year voyage in a thirty-six-foot longboat which had four sails and no engine.

He outraced bloodthirsty pirates off the coast of Morocco. He survived the fierce storms and dangerous currents off Cape Horn (at the tip of South America). He conquered the huge waves off the Cape of Good Hope (at the tip of Africa). He came into contact with sharks, whales, dolphins, unfriendly natives, and coral reefs.

Slocum was the most able and skilled seaman of his time. So it was nothing less than shocking when he and *The Spray* disappeared in 1909 on a short voyage to the Caribbean.

It had become a yearly tradition for Slocum to sail *The Spray* alone to the warm, tropical islands each fall. For Slocum, it was an easy trip. He left Martha's Vineyard, Massachusetts on November 14,

1909, bound for Grand Cayman Island. He and *The Spray* were never seen or heard from again.

There are a number of possible explanations for Slocum's disappearance. Did he vanish in a horrible storm at sea? Many felt there was no weather too terrible for the captain to deal with.

What was the condition of *The Spray*? Slocum had complete faith in his boat. Others said it was Slocum's skill, not the boat, that carried him through difficult situations in the past. They claimed *The Spray* was unstable and showed signs of age.

What about Slocum himself? His son, Victor, said he was in the best of health. But he was sixty-six years old and admitted to having blackouts now and then. He may have had a blackout or dizzy spell and fallen overboard. He could have slipped, been knocked unconscious, or had a heart attack.

Was there a fire on board *The Spray*? Most felt that Captain Slocum would have been very cautious with his stove and oil lamps. He was too experienced to be careless about a fire at sea.

Victor Slocum believed there was a collision at night with another, larger ship. In 1909 ships had no radar equipment. The area in which *The Spray* was sailing was well traveled by all kinds of ships.

At night, *The Spray* used oil-fired running lights, which were not very bright. Sometimes these were hidden from sight by the boat's sails. Slocum kept a torch nearby to light quickly but he might not have had the chance.

The lookout on a larger ship may have failed to see *The Spray* in the darkness and fog. Such a vessel could have easily run down and crushed *The Spray* without anyone ever knowing it.

Then there are those who claimed they saw Captain Slocum and *The Spray after* he was supposed to have vanished. Was he unhappy at home and did he disappear on purpose?

No trace was ever found of Joshua Slocum or his boat. It will always be one of the great mysteries of the sea. But he will forever be remembered as one of the most skillful and bravest sailors of all time.

Amelia Earhart

❧ 1937 ❧

She was known throughout the world as America's famous "First Lady of the Air." In 1932 Amelia Earhart became the only woman to fly across the Atlantic Ocean alone.

The greatest ambition of her career in aviation was to fly around the world. The trip was scheduled for May of 1937 when Amelia was thirty-nine years old.

On May 20, A.E. (as her friends called her) and navigator Fred Noonan took off from Oakland, California in a twin-engine Lockheed 10-E Electra airplane. They headed east to Tucson, Arizona; New Orleans, Louisiana; and Miami, Florida. Then the Electra flew on to Puerto Rico, Venezuela, Dutch Guiana, and Brazil.

On across the Atlantic they flew, through French West Africa, the Sudan, and Ethiopia. Then they crossed the Arabian Sea to India, Indonesia, Australia, and New Guinea.

People everywhere were following the flight of

Amelia Earhart and Fred Noonan. Each day newspapers carried articles about their progress. They had flown twenty-two thousand miles in forty days, made thirty stops in nineteen countries over five continents.

The most dangerous part of the trip was the twenty-six hundred miles of open ocean from New Guinea to Howland Island. It was the longest open crossing ever attempted.

Howland Island was a small dot (only 1½ miles long and ½ mile wide) in a huge ocean. It was a difficult place to find even with an expert navigator like Fred Noonan.

Noonan planned to take position fixes from the stars at night and the sun during the day to get them to Howland. Their radio, with a 50-watt transmitter, was limited. As they got closer to Howland, they expected to pick up signals from the Coast Guard cutter, *Itasca*. The ship was waiting to guide them in with a high frequency radio-direction finder.

Despite being nearly exhausted, the two took off from Lae, New Guinea on July 2, at 10:00 A.M. The Electra's speed would be more than 150 miles per hour. Noonan estimated the flight would take twenty hours. They had enough fuel for about twenty-four hours.

Lae was able to keep contact with the Electra for the first twelve hundred miles. All was going well. But the signal faded and they were out of contact for many hours until they got closer to the *Itasca*.

At 2:45 A.M. the next morning, the Coast Guard was able to pick up Amelia's voice through heavy static. "Cloudy and overcast" was all they heard. At 3:45 A.M. a garbled message came in saying she would listen for a signal. The *Itasca* tried and failed to make contact with the Electra.

It wasn't until 6:15 A.M. that the crew of the *Itasca* heard Amelia's voice, loud and clear, "We are about a hundred miles out. Please take a bearing on us and report in half an hour."

But the *Itasca* couldn't get a bearing. For over an hour, the crew tried repeatedly to contact the Electra but couldn't. Was Amelia receiving any messages at all?

Finally at 7:42 A.M. they heard a woman's voice, "We must be right on top of you, but we can't see you. Our gas is running low. Have been unable to reach you by radio . . . please take a bearing."

Itasca again tried to contact the Electra. It was obvious that the flyers were not receiving messages. "We're circling but cannot hear you," said Amelia at 8:00 A.M. when they were due to arrive at Howland. They had been in the air for twenty-two hours now.

The Coast Guard sent a long, continuous signal and finally Amelia responded, ". . . receiving your signals, but unable to get a minimum. Please take a bearing . . ." But the *Itasca* couldn't get a fix on the Electra's position and Noonan couldn't get a fix on the *Itasca's* position.

No contact was made again until nearly 9:00 A.M. Amelia's voice finally broke through the static, "We are in a line of position 157–337 . . . we are running north and south. We have only a half-hour's fuel left and cannot see land."

As Amelia Earhart frantically tried to locate

Howland Island, the men on the *Itasca* did everything they could to make contact with her. One, two, and then three hours passed. They didn't want to believe that the Electra must have gone down into the sea after running out of fuel.

One of the largest, most expensive searches in history began. For sixteen days, 250,000 square miles of ocean was searched around Howland Island as well as the Gilbert and Marshall Islands. Planes and ships took part and not a trace was found of Amelia Earhart, Fred Noonan, or their aircraft.

The world was shocked. Americans were stunned. Amelia Earhart was dead . . . or was she? To this day, there are rumors and theories about what really happened to the First Lady of the Air.

Although the U.S. and Japan were at peace with each other in 1937, Americans suspected that the Japanese were making plans for war. Some believe that A.E. was on a secret spy mission for the United States government to photograph Japanese island installations in the Pacific. She and Noonan were either shot down by the Japanese or captured and then killed.

Others feel Amelia came down on a Japanese island by accident. She and Noonan were taken prisoner and sent to Saipan where they later died in prison or were executed as spies.

To this day, the Japanese deny these stories. But some believe they would never admit to such a thing since it was in violation of international law at the time. Did the U.S. government close the file on the case in the 1960s so as not to embarrass the Japanese?

Were the two flyers testing a supercharged experimental Air Force plane on a special mission? Were they rescued secretly and flown back to the States with new identities? Was their disappearance a government cover-up? Are they still alive today?

Or did Amelia Earhart and Fred Noonan drift off course and miss tiny Howland Island? They may have ditched the Electra in the sea and stayed afloat for several days until a storm overwhelmed them.

Others think that Amelia went on searching for Howland until the last possible second. Then, when the fuel ran out and the engines stopped, she aimed the Electra into the sea.

"Someday, I'll probably get killed," A.E. once said. "But when I do, I want to go in my plane quickly."

The last flight of Amelia Earhart is one of the great mysteries of the air.

Baychimo

❦ 1931 ❦

The *Baychimo* was a thirteen-hundred-ton steamer. She carried a crew of seventeen and operated in icy Arctic waters. The crew hunted animals for their pelts and these expensive furs were stowed in the ship's cargo area.

Built in 1921, the *Baychimo*'s home port was Vancouver, British Columbia. For ten years, the steamer traveled safely through dangerous waters filled with icebergs and floating sea ice.

In October 1931, the *Baychimo* got caught in a terrible blizzard. She was in the Arctic Ocean, west of Point Barrow, Alaska.

"We're caught tight in ice, Captain," said the first mate. "She can't move an inch."

"The pressure's too great on her hull. It might be crushed," said the captain, who ordered the crew to leave the ship and set up camp on the ice closer to shore.

"We won't let the *Baychimo* and those furs out

of our sight," he explained. "If we have to, we'll wait for better weather and a thaw in the ice."

"Or we'll wait until the *Baychimo* is crushed and sunk," thought the mate to himself.

Weeks passed and the steamer was still stuck tight. Finally temperatures warmed up slightly. One morning, the men woke up and found the ship had vanished.

"She must have broken free during the night," said the captain. "She's not in sight."

The crew made their way to Point Barrow. There, a hunter said he had spotted the *Baychimo* about fifty miles south of where they had last seen her.

Thinking they had a chance to save the steamer's valuable cargo, the crew, with the help of local Eskimos, traveled by dogsled and found the ship. It took them days to unload the furs which were worth nearly a million dollars. But before they had a chance to finish the job, the *Baychimo* disappeared again.

This time months passed before the ship was spotted. She was caught in ice east of Point Barrow, in MacKenzie Bay, near the Yukon Territory. The steamer had been boarded by gold prospectors who said she was still sound and in good condition. Whatever furs had been left were now gone.

The *Baychimo* took off again and it was over a year before it was sighted near Point Barrow in 1933. It was as if the steamer had a mind of its own!

In 1934 crewmen from another vessel boarded the *Baychimo* and found that she was now in poor condition. The weather had taken its toll on the drifting ship.

From then on, the ship was sighted year after year. Some sailors tried to tow her into port in 1939 for salvage, but bad weather stopped them. Soon after, she disappeared again.

Years passed and still the abandoned *Baychimo* drifted alone in the icy waters. It's a mystery that the ship wasn't damaged or crushed by the ice.

The last sighting of this ship that steered itself was in 1956. Some Eskimos saw her in the Beaufort Sea near eastern Alaska. She had been patrolling these waters alone for twenty-five years!

What finally happened to the *Baychimo*? She may have been destroyed long ago. But there's another possibility. The old ship may still be locked in ice somewhere in the frozen northern waters, just waiting for a spring thaw to set her free again.

Glossary

AGROUND: the bottom caught in the ground or on the shore

ARMOR: a protective covering of metal

BEARING: position or location

BOW: the forward part of a ship

BROADSIDE: the side of a ship above the water

COLLIER: a ship used to transport coal

COMPASS: an instrument for determining direction

DEBRIS: the remains of something which was destroyed

DECK: the platform on a ship forming the floor

DERELICT: abandoned by the owner

DISTRESS CALL: *see* Mayday or SOS

FLARE: a blazing light used to attract attention

FREQUENCY: electromagnetic waves (kilocycles to

megacycles) used in radio transmission, similar to channels

GALE: strong, gusty winds from 32 to 63 miles per hour

GALLEY: kitchen area of ship or airplane

HORIZON: where the earth and sky meet

HULL: the frame or body of a ship

MAST: a pole rising from the deck of a ship which supports the sails and lines

MAYDAY: signal word used as a call for help

METALLIC: like metal

MUTINY: revolt against officers

NAVIGATION: the science of getting ships and planes from place to place by determining course, position, and distance

PIRACY: robbery on the high seas

PORT: the left side of a ship or airplane, when facing forward

QUARTERDECK: the rear area of a ship's upper deck, used by officers and captain

REEF: chain of rocks or sand near the surface of the water

RIGGINGS: lines used aboard a ship

SALVAGE: money paid for saving a ship and its cargo

SEAWORTHY: safe for a sea voyage

SOS: a signal for help in radio code

SQUID: a 10-armed cephalopod, similar to an octopus

STARBOARD: the right side of a ship or airplane, when facing forward

STEAMER: a boat powered by steam

STERN: the rear end of a ship

WATERSPOUT: a funnel-shaped sea tornado

WIRELESS: radio telegraph